Battles of the American Revolution
Saratoga

VICTORIA RUSHWORTH

Table of Contents

Introduction 2
Chapter 1 The Stage is Set 4
Chapter 2 A Good Beginning 7
Chapter 3 Moving On 11
Chapter 4 The Battles 20
Conclusion 28
Solve This Answers 30
Glossary 31
Index 32

Introduction

September 19th, 1777. October 7th, 1777. These two dates were crucial in the American Revolutionary War. On these dates General John Burgoyne and his army of British, German, and Canadian soldiers clashed with American troops under the leadership of Major General Horatio Gates. Both battles took place near the small town of Saratoga, New York, north of Albany, New York.

During these two battles, the Americans showed the world what they were worth. Although the British forces won the first battle of Saratoga, they suffered about twice as many casualties as the Americans. The Americans fought back during the second battle of Saratoga, and with grim determination and superior numbers of men, won the day. The British surrendered.

▼ Saratoga National Historical Park, NY

The Battles of Saratoga

Dates: September 19th, 1777–October 17th, 1777
Locations: Freeman's Farm, outside Saratoga, New York
Bemis Heights, outside Saratoga, New York
Weather: Mild, cloudy, rainy

American Leaders:
General Horatio Gates
General Benedict Arnold
Colonel Daniel Morgan

British Leaders:
General John Burgoyne
Baron Friedrich Riedesel
General Simon Fraser

American Casualties:
800 killed, wounded, and missing

British Casualties:
1,600 killed, wounded, and missing
6,000 surrendered

Before the American victory at Saratoga, France had been supplying the American rebels with weapons. When news of the British surrender at Saratoga reached France, that country entered a pact to commit full military and financial support to America and its cause. The British were now at war not only with America, but with France and its allies, Spain and Holland.

In this book, you will follow the British and American troops in the months and days leading up to the battles of Saratoga. You will be with the officers and soldiers during the two momentous battles. On your journey, consider what factors led to the outcomes of the battles of Saratoga.

CHAPTER 1

The Stage Is Set

In December 1777, General John Burgoyne of Great Britain was home. He had just returned from fighting the American rebels in Canada. He had been successful in battle. He was determined to go back to fight again. And he had a plan. His idea was to cut off the rebels in the North. He would cut the New England states off from the rest of the country. On paper, the plan looked like a good idea. But in reality, it would prove much harder to execute.

Burgoyne's idea was to divide his army into three columns, or groups. Burgoyne would lead the main column south from Canada into America. He would travel down the Hudson River. A second column would be led by General William Howe.

The column would march north from New York City. The two columns would meet in Albany, New York. Meanwhile, a third column, led by Lieutenant Colonel Barry St. Leger, would travel from Canada down the Mohawk River. The rebels then would have to fight the British on the banks of the Hudson and Mohawk Rivers. St. Leger planned to capture rebel-held Fort Stanwix, and then move on to Albany.

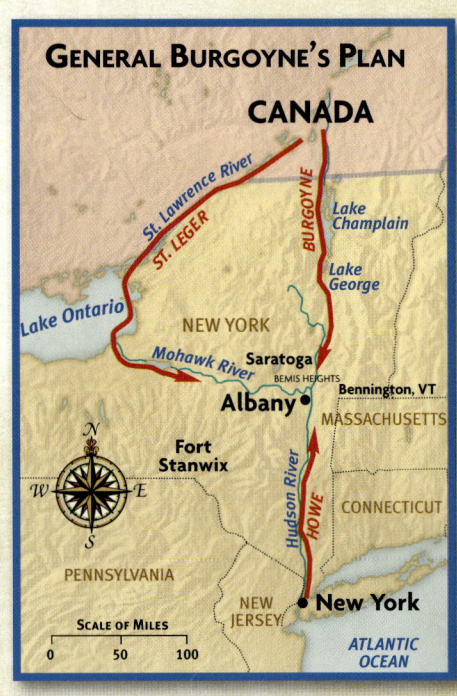

▲ Burgoyne divided his army into three columns.

4

LEADERS OF THE FIGHT

General John Burgoyne was born in London on February 24, 1722. When he was fifteen, he joined the army. Burgoyne earned a reputation as a gambler. He also loved the theater and liked to write. One of his plays was produced on the London stage.

At the age of twenty-eight, he married the daughter of an earl. Her family did not approve. Her father would not give them any money. Burgoyne's salary could barely cover his gambling debts. So he sold his commission to raise money. In those days, officers had to buy a commission in the army. Later, Burgoyne was able to buy himself a place in the army again. Burgoyne was sent to Boston, Massachusetts, to fight the American rebels. He was there for the Battle of Bunker Hill. Afterward, he returned to England.

In 1777, King George III agreed to send Burgoyne back to Canada with close to 7,000 troops to fight in the Revolution. After his defeat at Saratoga, Burgoyne went home to London. He lived the rest of his life quietly. He started writing again and even wrote a successful play. Burgoyne died in London on June 4, 1792.

CHAPTER 1

SOLDIERS OF THE WAR

The German soldiers who fought in the American Revolution were known as "Hessians." The soldiers were hired by the British, who simply did not have enough soldiers of their own. British regulars were on duty in Ireland, the West Indies, and other countries in the British Empire. Some 20,000 German soldiers served in the American Revolution. The first German king to offer troops was Friedrich II of Hesse-Cassel. That is where the term "Hessian" comes from. The official name of the soldiers was **Brunswickers**.

▲ Hessian soldiers

But Burgoyne's plan didn't consider one very important factor: the wilderness. The **terrain** was rough. It was mountainous, and the land was covered with thick forests.

Most of the region was still unsettled. The distances between towns was great. The British did not fully understand just how big America was.

But at the time, none of that concerned General Burgoyne. He was determined to achieve his goal. As soon as King George III agreed with the plan, General Burgoyne set sail for Canada. With him were 7,000 troops, including **Hessian** soldiers.

CHAPTER 2

A Good Beginning

Burgoyne set off from Canada in June of 1777. He had with him about 9,000 men. Four thousand of them were "British regulars." Four thousand more were Germans. The rest were Canadians and Indians. The Indians would serve as scouts and guide Burgoyne's troops through the wilderness.

The going was not easy. The men had to cut roads out of the forest and build bridges. The Americans did not make it any easier. Whenever they were forced to move, they burned crops and houses. They took livestock with them or set the animals free. They destroyed bridges and cut down trees to block roads.

WOMEN OF THE WAR

Many of the ships that crossed the Atlantic with Burgoyne included women. It was not unusual for women to travel with the troops. Each army had women to cook for them and do laundry. Wives of both regular soldiers and officers followed their men into battle. One such woman was Lady Harriet Acland. She was the wife of a major who fought at Saratoga. Her husband was wounded and taken prisoner by the Americans. Even though she was pregnant, Lady Harriet crossed the river to the enemy camp at night. She asked permission to nurse her husband. American general Horatio Gates allowed her to do so.

CHAPTER 2

A TURN OF EVENTS

British troops had laid **siege** to Fort Stanwix, in an effort to force the Americans to surrender. But American general Benedict Arnold caused the British to retreat.

Burgoyne learned about the setback at Fort Stanwix. But he had heard nothing from General Howe, whose troops were supposed to be marching north from New York City.

Supplies were running low. Burgoyne decided to send soldiers into Vermont to get fresh supplies and more horses. By then, rebel soldiers were pouring into Vermont.

They Made a Difference

▲ Colonel Barry St. Leger

Benedict Arnold convinced the British to give up Fort Stanwix through a trick. He made a deal with an American man named Hon Yost. Yost was a **Loyalist**, who had been captured by the Americans. Yost had to convince the Indians fighting with the British that a huge rebel force was marching toward them. If he did, he could go free. Yost did a good job. The Indians believed him and took off into the forest. Without the Indians to help him fight, St. Leger retreated. It was all a trick. There never was a huge army of rebels.

A GOOD BEGINNING

"The moment is a decisive one."
–General Burgoyne on his decision to march to Albany at all costs

At Bennington, Vermont, Burgoyne's troops were badly beaten by American **militia** units. The general lost over 200 men. Another 700 were taken prisoner. Only forty Americans were killed and thirty wounded. Burgoyne failed to get his supplies.

But in spite of the odds, Burgoyne was determined to keep moving forward.

Solve This

General Burgoyne's 9,000 men had enough food to last thirty days. Each man consumed one half pound of food per day. How many pounds of food were required to feed the men for thirty days?

Historical Perspective

In colonial wartime, food was a big concern. Food did not stay fresh very long. It was hard to find more. Soldiers carried flour to make their own bread. Today's armies carry food that has been canned or freeze-dried. It can last for months.

CHAPTER 2

They Made a Difference

The troops that fought in the Revolution were from state militias and the Continental army. The militias had existed in the colonies since before the war. When they were needed, those men would defend their own territory. They usually signed up for a short time and then returned home. All during the war this was a problem for the officers in charge.

No matter where he was, even in the middle of battle, when a man's time was up, he could simply leave. On the one hand, this made sense. Most of the men in the militias were farmers. They were needed at home to grow food. No food at home meant no food for the troops.

▲ Continental army soldier

The Continental army was created by Congress after the Battle of Bunker Hill. It was commanded by George Washington. Most of the time, men enlisted for a year or two. Many deserted because Congress could not pay them or feed them.

CHAPTER 3

Moving On

General Burgoyne had to make a choice. There were two ways to get to Albany. Both were dangerous.

Burgoyne could continue along the east bank of the Hudson River. There were not likely to be many rebel troops on the east side of the river. Then he could cross the Hudson River below where the Hudson and the Mohawk Rivers joined. But the river was wide and deep there, and American soldiers and their cannons would be in the hills above the river. The British soldiers that did make it across the river would then have to climb the steep banks along the river. They would be climbing right into the line of enemy fire.

The other choice was to cross the Hudson first and then go down the west side of the river. The crossing would be easier. But then Burgoyne would be fighting his way through American troops the entire way to Albany. And Albany was 45 miles away.

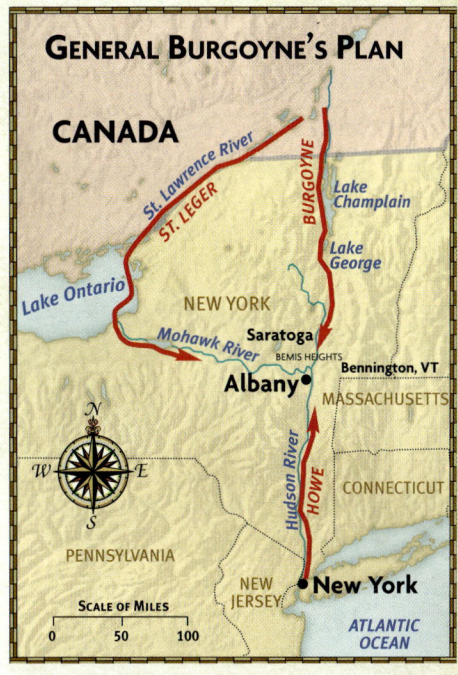

▲ Burgoyne's march to Albany

Solve This

Each wagon Burgoyne had with him could hold 2,500 pounds of food. How many wagons did General Burgoyne need to transport one month's worth of rations? (Use the answer from the first Solve This on page 9.)

11

CHAPTER 3

British Uniforms

1768 clothing warrant – Regulations for the Clothing of Marching Regiments of the Foot

HATS
The hats were laced either with gold or silver.

EPAULETTES
The Officers of **grenadiers** wore an epaulette on each shoulder. They were either of embroidery or lace, with gold or silver fringe.

CAPS FOR GRENADIER OFFICERS
The Officers of the grenadiers wore black bear-skin caps.

UNIFORM OF OFFICERS
The number of each regiment was on the buttons of the uniforms of the Officers and men.

WAISTCOATS
The waistcoats were plain, without either embroidery or lace.

SWORDS
The swords of each regiment were uniform. The hilts were either gilt or silver, according to the color of the buttons on the uniforms.

CARTRIDGE BOX
Each side of the box held 18 rounds of ammunition.

12

MOVING ON

American Uniforms
Second Massachusetts Regiment of Continental Infantry, 1777

Unlike the British, the American soldiers were not all dressed alike. For one thing, the soldiers came from different militias. And there was little money for fancy uniforms.

Before 1779, there was no regulation uniform for the Massachusetts regiments in Continental service. But most Massachusetts soldiers who had uniforms wore blue coats faced and lined with white.

The regiments were recognized by the numbers stamped on the pewter buttons.

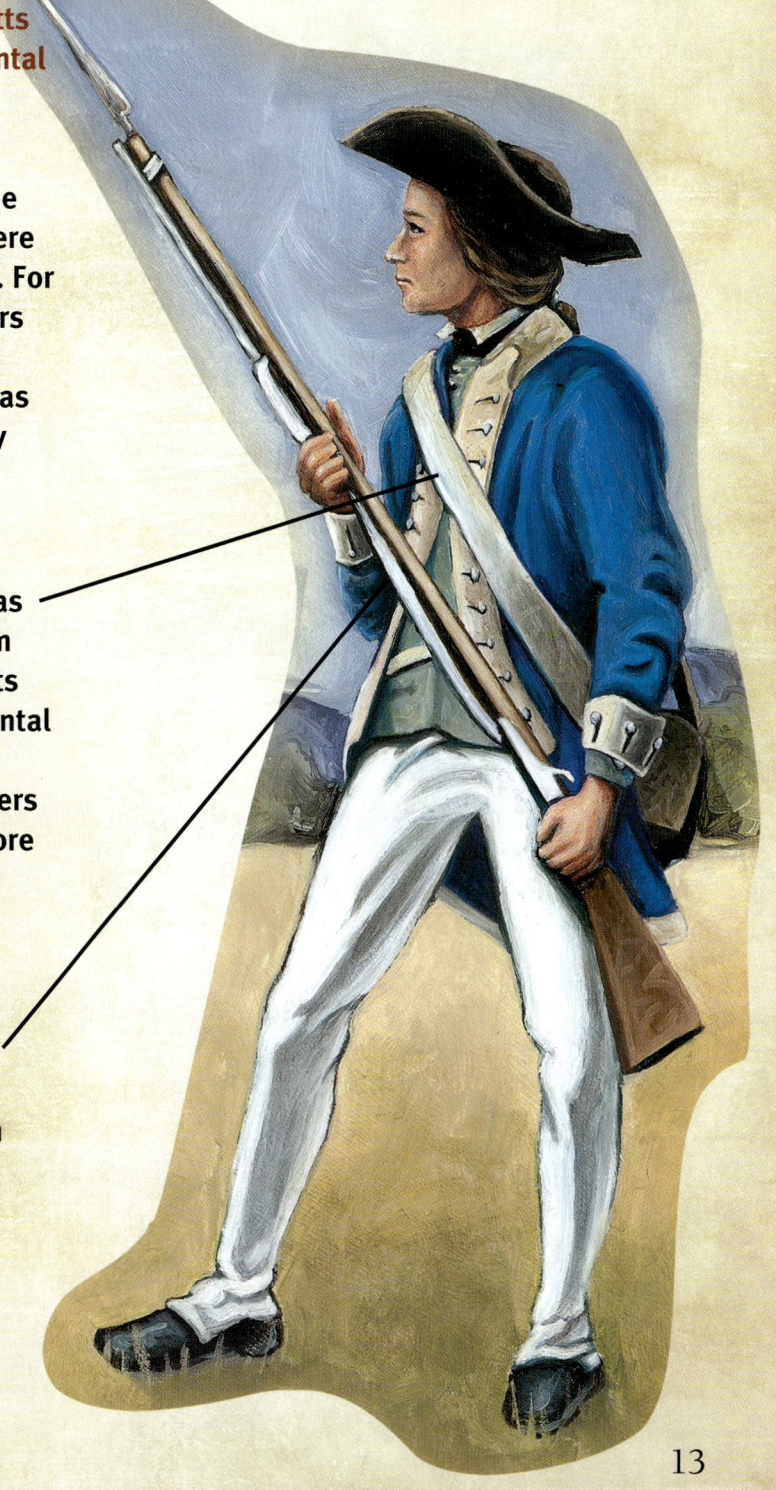

13

CHAPTER 3

A CHOICE IS MADE

Burgoyne made his decision. His army would cross the Hudson River first. Then they would march down the west bank of the river. September 13, 1777, was a bright, sunny day. General Burgoyne's men had enough **provisions** to last for four weeks. They had to reach Albany in one month. If not, they might starve, or worse, face defeat. On that sunny morning, Burgoyne marched his troops across the river. They walked across a bridge made of boats tied together. Two days later, General Riedesel and the German soldiers followed.

3 Solve This

Each one of General Burgoyne's wagons was drawn by two horses. How many horses were required to pull all the wagons? (Use the answer from the second Solve This on page 11.)

THEY MADE A DIFFERENCE

Friedrich Adolph Riedesel was in charge of the German soldiers who fought alongside General Burgoyne.

He was born in 1738 into a German noble family. He left home at age fifteen to study. At school, he loved to watch the Hesse troops drill. When he was seventeen, a friend told Riedesel his father had given him permission to become a soldier. But it was a lie.

When the Duke of Brunswick agreed to "rent" soldiers to the British during the Revolutionary War, it was Major General Riedesel who was put in charge. Riedesel and his family arrived in Canada in June of 1777.

After the war, Riedesel returned to Germany. He arrived home with less than half of the soldiers that he had set out with. Riedesel died at home on January 6, 1800.

MOVING ON

Once Riedesel and his men had crossed the Hudson, the boats were untied. Burgoyne had decided his fate. A return to Canada was no longer an option.

The soldiers marched in three columns. The **artillery**, the guns and ammunition, were in the middle. On the right were the British troops, led by General Burgoyne. General Riedesel and his Brunswickers marched on the left, next to the river. They were 6,500 in total. But the army that stepped off that September morning was weary. They were hungry, ragged, and tired of war. And they knew that American forces might be waiting for them at every turn.

It's a Fact

The army was not alone. Burgoyne's troops were joined by hundreds of camp followers. These included members of the clergy, doctors, women, and children. Officers had servants. General Riedesel's wife even had her own carriage.

▲ Baroness Riedesel and family

CHAPTER 3

THE AMERICANS PREPARE

General Burgoyne set up camp at Saratoga to begin his **campaign**. Meanwhile, American troops under the command of Major General Horatio Gates were camped at Stillwater, New York, south of Saratoga. The American troops were preparing for battle.

> **Primary Source**
>
> "... an aide-de-camp showed me a fresh scalp-lock which I could not mistake."
> —Jane McCrae's fiancé

WOMEN OF THE WAR

The murder of an American woman was used as **propaganda** to excite rebels against the British. Jane McCrae lived in Saratoga with one of her brothers. At the start of the war, two of her brothers joined the American forces. But the man she was to marry was a Loyalist. He went to Canada to join the British. He became a soldier in Burgoyne's army. Jane was on her way to meet him when she and another woman were captured by a band of Indians who were fighting with the British.

▲ Jane McCrae

There are different stories about what happened next. But one way or another, Jane was murdered by her captors and scalped. The scalps were taken to Burgoyne's camp. There, McCrae's fiancé recognized her hair. McCrae is buried near Fort Edward in New York. In 2003, her body was exhumed. Experts hoped to learn more about her death, but they did not.

MOVING ON

SOLDIERS OF THE WAR

Horatio Gates was born in England in 1728. His parents were servants. As a young man, he joined the British army. He fought in the French and Indian Wars in America. Gates resigned from the British Army in 1772. He retired to live in Virginia. But his military career was only beginning. He soon became involved in the rebel cause. As soon as the Revolution started, Gates joined up. His first major command was to head up the Northern department of the war. He took over on August 19th, just in time for Saratoga.

Gates is famous for his victory over Burgoyne. But he was never on the battlefield. In fact, he never left his headquarters.

After Saratoga, Gates continued to serve. But he was never again a winning commander. In fact, he was accused of leaving the scene of battle and was investigated. Nothing came of it. Gates retired from army life in 1784. He moved to New York where he died in 1806.

General Horatio Gates ▶

CHAPTER 3

Gates now had soldiers from New York, Massachusetts, New Jersey, New Hampshire, Connecticut, and Pennsylvania. More men poured into camp every day. In all there were close to 10,000. One of the most important men was Daniel Morgan.

Morgan led the Virginia riflemen. His men were crack shots and scouts. They could creep through the woods as quietly as any Indian scout the British used.

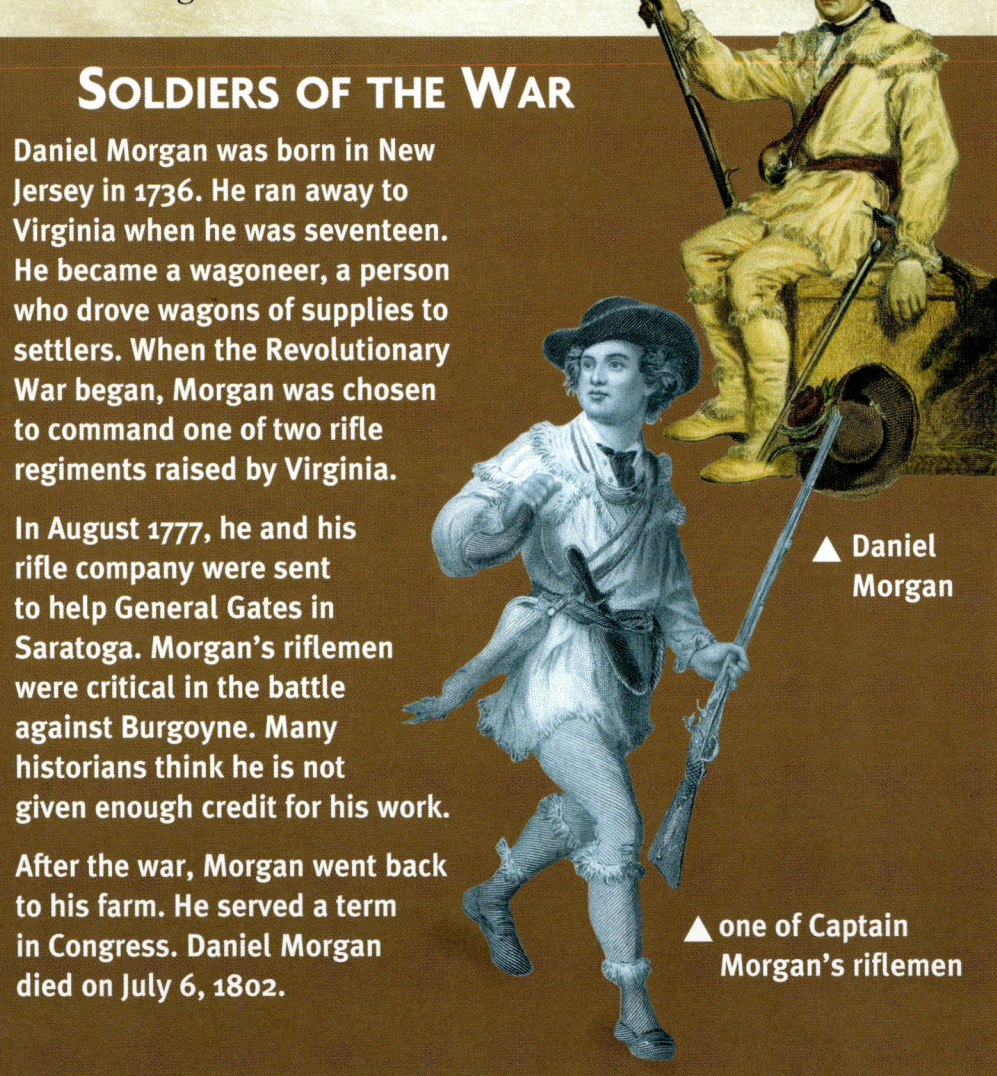

SOLDIERS OF THE WAR

Daniel Morgan was born in New Jersey in 1736. He ran away to Virginia when he was seventeen. He became a wagoneer, a person who drove wagons of supplies to settlers. When the Revolutionary War began, Morgan was chosen to command one of two rifle regiments raised by Virginia.

In August 1777, he and his rifle company were sent to help General Gates in Saratoga. Morgan's riflemen were critical in the battle against Burgoyne. Many historians think he is not given enough credit for his work.

After the war, Morgan went back to his farm. He served a term in Congress. Daniel Morgan died on July 6, 1802.

▲ Daniel Morgan

▲ one of Captain Morgan's riflemen

MOVING ON

Once Gates's troops had made camp, they were sent out to scout the area. They needed a suitable place to meet the enemy. The local people all recommended Bemis Heights, about nine miles (14.5 kilometers) south of Saratoga.

It was perfect. The broad **plateau** was thickly wooded. It was higher than the land around it. From the plateau, a soldier could see for miles in every direction.

Below the heights was a cleared passage of land. The only road to Albany ran through the passage. It was the road Burgoyne would soon come marching down.

It's a Fact

Bemis Heights was named after Jotham Bemis, a man who kept a tavern nearby.

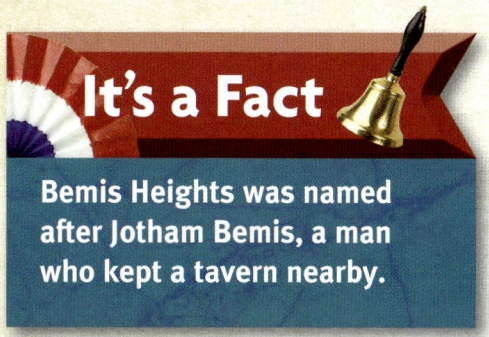
▼ Bemis Heights

CHAPTER 4

The Battles

General Burgoyne had seen the rebels at Bemis Heights. But he did not know what Gates had planned. The Indian scouts that were with him when he left Canada had deserted. But he did know one thing: The only road to Albany would go right past Bemis Heights.

General Gates did not have a much better idea of the British plans. He sent Daniel Morgan and his men out to scout the enemy. But Morgan was not familiar with the territory. He had trouble finding his way at first. Gates knew Burgoyne had to move soon. Both sides knew battle was only days, or even hours, away.

SEPTEMBER 19: BATTLE DAY

Dawn arrived on Friday, September 19, with a cold, gray fog. The thick fog made it hard to see. As the morning wore on and the air began to clear, American scouts caught sight of movement in the British camp.

▲ British soldiers

 **POINT**

Picture It
Reread pages 20–21. Imagine you are an American scout. What would you have seen when the fog cleared?

The British began to move out. They broke into three columns. One column moved far out to the right. Led by General Simon Fraser, those soldiers would cover the advance of the main army.

The left column, led by General Riedesel, would march up from the river. They controlled all the heavy artillery, light and heavy cannons, and guns. The main army would march down the middle. General Burgoyne and his staff would ride with the main force.

Gates was willing to wait and see what Burgoyne had in mind. But not General Benedict Arnold.

Arnold was known for being hotheaded. He was always ready to take action. Under Arnold's orders, Morgan and his men marched to the woods. They climbed trees to wait for the enemy.

▲ Benedict Arnold

CHAPTER 4

"Both armies seemed determined to conquer or die."
–General Clover

SHOTS ARE FIRED

At about 1:00 in the afternoon, 300 British soldiers appeared over a hill. They entered a clearing known as Freeman's Farm. When they came into sight, Morgan's riflemen fired. Almost at once, the front line dropped to the ground. Excited at their success, the riflemen ran from the cover of the trees to attack the soldiers. It was a fatal mistake. General Fraser's men arrived and began to fire. The riflemen were hit from the side.

Gates ordered more soldiers to the field to help Morgan. Now rebels and British were face to face on the battlefield.

Primary Source

One American soldier described the guns firing without stop. He called it, "the hottest fire of cannon . . . that I ever heard in my life."

THE BATTLES

It's a Fact

When Burgoyne and Clinton needed to get in touch with each other, they sent coded letters. The letters were meant to be read through a cutout shaped like an hourglass. The technique was not new. It had been invented in the 16th century by a man named Geronimo Cardano.

Sir Henry Clinton ▶

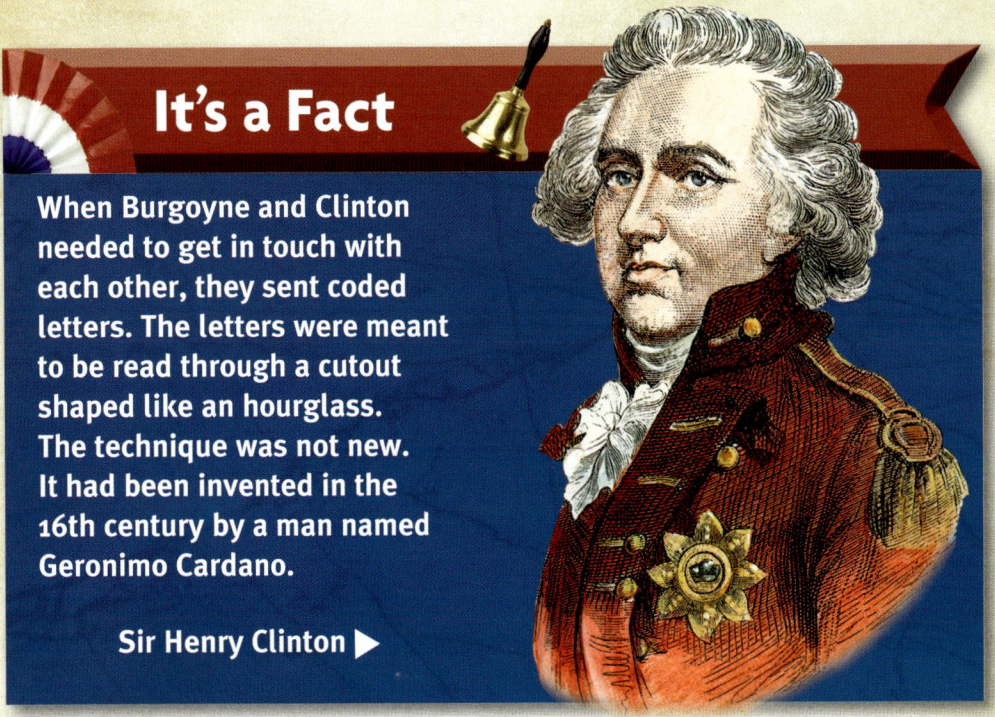

The fighting raged on for hours. First one side seemed to be winning, then the other. Soon the dead and dying were everywhere.

As darkness fell, the Americans retreated. The British had not been driven from the field. They had won the day. But there was no reason for celebration. General Burgoyne had lost 160 men. Another 364 were wounded and 42 were missing. The Americans had just over 300 casualties.

General Burgoyne had lost about 300 more men than General Gates had. And even on the day of the battle, new American troops continued to arrive.

A LETTER OF FALSE HOPE

On September 21, a letter arrived for General Burgoyne. It was from Sir Henry Clinton, commander of British forces in New York City. Clinton let Burgoyne know that he expected to arrive with more men in about ten days.

CHAPTER 4

Burgoyne decided to wait for Clinton's troops. The wait was brutal. More than 700 soldiers lay sick. Every day more men died. There were not enough blankets or tents. Many soldiers slept on the bare ground. That is, if they slept at all. Men were on constant guard duty looking out for the Americans.

Meanwhile, General Gates was also waiting. He knew Burgoyne was probably running low on supplies and food. And Gates himself was low on ammunition.

Nearly three weeks passed. Time was running out. Burgoyne had to press on. He could not wait for Clinton's troops. On October 4th, he called his generals to a council of war.

General Horatio Gates ▶

OCTOBER 7: ONE LAST STAND

The decision was made. Burgoyne would attack again. He planned to leave 800 men on the river to guard the supplies that were left, and the hospital. The rest would move through the woods to attack Gates.

But Burgoyne's generals did not agree with him. General Riedesel thought it was foolish to risk all the men on one mission. Burgoyne gave in and agreed to send out 2,000 men.

THE BATTLES

**THE BATTLE OF SARATOGA
October 7, 1777**

Their job was to spy on the enemy to see how strong it was. If an attack seemed possible, they would march the next day. If not, they would retreat.

At 1:00 P.M. the soldiers were finally ready to march. Once again, Burgoyne divided his soldiers. On the right were Fraser and his men. On the left were British and German grenadiers. In the center was General Riedesel. The Americans were ready. They attacked. General Fraser was badly wounded. The British tried to retreat. But General Benedict Arnold would not allow it.

25

CHAPTER 4

Arnold had been ordered by Gates to stay away. But instead he rushed out, grabbed a horse, and charged onto the battlefield. He took command of the troops and attacked fiercely. His courage and determination won the day for the Americans. Again and again he rode across the battle lines. He only stopped when he was shot in the leg. Arnold's horse fell and he was pinned beneath him.

For the British, the end was in sight. They began to retreat to Saratoga. Baroness Riedesel was among the men and women who retreated. Her diary gives a vivid account of the march back to Saratoga.

It's a Fact

At Saratoga there is a monument to Benedict Arnold's leg.

SOLDIERS OF THE WAR

Had Benedict Arnold died on the battlefield at Saratoga, he would be remembered today as a hero. But later in the war, he became a spy for the British. He planned to hand the keys to the fort at West Point to the British. But the plot was uncovered. Arnold managed to escape to England. He died there in 1801. His place in history is as a traitor, not a hero.

▲ Benedict Arnold

THE BATTLES

Primary Source

Baroness Riedesel
The Defeat and Surrender of Burgoyne

"On the 9th, it rained terribly the whole day; nevertheless we kept ourselves ready to march. We reached Saratoga about dark... I was quite wet, and was obliged to remain in that condition, for want of a place to change my apparel. I seated myself near the fire, and undressed the children, and we then laid ourselves upon some straw. I refreshed myself at 7 o'clock, the next morning (the 10th of October), with a cup of tea. About 2 o'clock, we heard again a report of muskets and cannon... My husband sent me word, that I should immediately retire into a house which was not far off. Soon after our arrival, a terrible cannonade began, and... We were at last obliged to descend into the cellar... I laid myself in a corner near the door. My children put their heads upon my knees. An abominable smell, the cries of the children, and my own anguish of mind, did not permit me to close my eyes, during the whole night. On the next morning, the cannonade begun anew... Eleven cannon-balls passed through the house."

 POINT

Think About It
Reread page 27. What do you think the Baroness was thinking during the siege?

27

Conclusion

In October 17th, on the banks of the Hudson River at Saratoga, General Burgoyne surrendered to General Gates. The two men rode up to each other. They got off their horses and General Burgoyne handed his sword to General Gates. Gates held it for a moment and then returned it to Burgoyne. Next, the men of the ranks were to meet. Under the terms of the surrender, the British and German troops would march out of camp "with the honors of war."

Column by column, the 6,000 men passed by the American troops and marched to a place on the riverbank where they surrendered their weapons. As the enemy marched by, the Americans stood in complete silence.

THE TURNING POINT

The battles of Saratoga changed the course of the American Revolution. The Americans, under the

▲ the surrender

leadership of General Horatio Gates, had defeated the greatest military power in the world: Great Britain.

As a result of the events at Saratoga, France and her allies Spain and Holland agreed to join the war on the American side. With their help, the fate of Great Britain was sealed. The end came with the surrender at Yorktown in 1781. The American Revolution was over. America was a free country.

The brave men and women on both sides at Saratoga fought for what they believed in. But in the end, the Americans had more to fight for: freedom. As soldier Henry Dearborn wrote, "We . . . had something more at stake than fighting for sixpence per day."

It's a Fact

As the British and German soldiers marched to surrender, they were trailed by the camp followers. Along with these men and women was a collection of deer, raccoons, and other wild animals who had become their pets.

4 Solve This

On average, members of the American militia were paid sixpence (about one nickel) per day. If the average term of enlistment was two months, (60 days) how much did a soldier earn?

Solve This Answers

Solve This 1 (Page 9)
135,000 pounds of food for thirty days

Solve This 2 (Page 11)
54 wagons

Solve This 3 (Page 14)
108 horses

Solve This 4 (Page 29)
60 days x .05 = $3.00 for two months' work

Glossary

artillery — (ar-TIH-ler-ee) heavy, cart-drawn guns and cannons (page 15)

Brunswicker — (BRUNZ-wik-er) another name for a Hessian or German soldier (page 6)

campaign — (kam-PANE) a series of military operations with a specific goal (page 16)

grenadier — (greh-nuh-DEER) a British soldier who threw grenades and made bombs (page 12)

Hessian — (HEH-shun) a German soldier who fought with the British in the American Revolution (page 6)

Loyalist — (LOY-uh-list) an American colonist who remained loyal to the king of England (page 8)

militia — (mih-LIH-shuh) an army of volunteer citizens organized during an emergency (page 9)

plateau — (pla-TOH) an elevated piece of land with a level surface (page 19)

propaganda — (prah-puh-GAN-duh) material designed to influence the opinion of a person or group (page 16)

provisions — (pruh-VIH-zhunz) the food and drink carried by a soldier (page 14)

siege — (SEEJ) constant and continuous battle over a specific place (page 8)

terrain — (tuh-RANE) another name for the type of land—wooded, or mountainous, for example—in an area (page 6)

Index

Acland, Lady Harriet, 7
Arnold, General Benedict, 3, 8, 21, 25–26
artillery, 15, 21
Bemis Heights, 19–20
Brunswickers, 6, 15
Burgoyne, General John, 2–9, 11, 14–21, 23–25, 27–28
campaign, 16
Clinton, Sir Henry, 23–24
Fort Stanwix, 4, 8
Fraser, General Simon, 3, 21–22
Freeman's Farm 3, 22
Gates, General Horatio, 2–3, 7, 16–24, 26, 28–29
grenadiers, 12, 25
Hessians, 6
Howe, General William, 4, 8
Hudson River, 11, 14–15, 28
Indian, 7–8, 16, 18, 20

King Friedrich II, 6
King George III, 5–6
Loyalist, 8, 16
McCrae, Jane, 16
militia, 9–10, 29
Mohawk River, 4, 11
Morgan, Colonel Daniel, 3, 18, 21–22
plateau, 19
propaganda, 16
provisions, 14
Riedesel, Baron Friedrich, 3, 14–15
Riedesel, Baroness, 15, 26–27
St. Leger, Lt. Colonel, 4, 8
siege, 8, 27
terrain, 6
Virginia riflemen, 14, 22
Washington, General George, 10